IT'S A
BOY!

MARIANNE RICHMOND

Published by Sourcebooks, Inc.
P.O. Box 4410, Naperville, Illinois 60567-4410
(630) 961-3900
Fax: (630) 961-2168
www.sourcebooks.com

Printed and bound in China.

LEO 10 9 8 7 6 5 4 3 2

To: _____

From: _____

What a wonderful blessing.

His ten
tiny fingers.

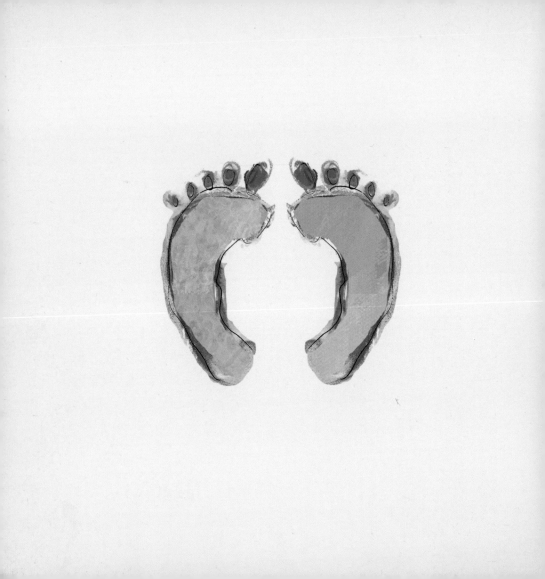

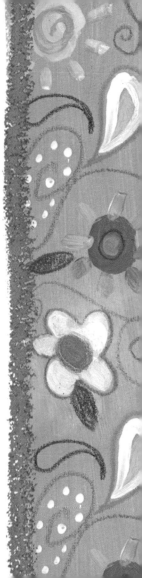

Sweet, kissable toes.

Chubby, cherubic cheeks
and cute button nose.

Did you ever think

someone so *little*

could make you feel love…

so
BIG?

Delight in the "boy-ness" of it all.

Baby blue sleepers.
Miniature overalls.
Dots, stripes, and plaids.

Cars, trucks,

and balls.

There is nothing so innocent
and so heartwarming…

...as little boy playtime.

Chasing frogs,
looking for caterpillars,
and playing in anything
muddy or "puddle-y."

He'll endear you with
his crazy, colicky hair,

scrapes, bumps,
and bruises,

Kool-Aid kisses
and everyday muses.

Boys love speed.

From crawling
to walking.

From running
to riding.

From taking the dare…

to being the dare devil.

Hold your breath!

Boys are tough on the outside.

And so soft on the inside.

Make time for him.

Listen to him.

Celebrate him.

Pray for him.

Kiss him often.

Hug him tightly.
(But not in front of his friends.)

And love him unconditionally.

Teach him kindness
and manners
and feelings
and self-sufficiency.

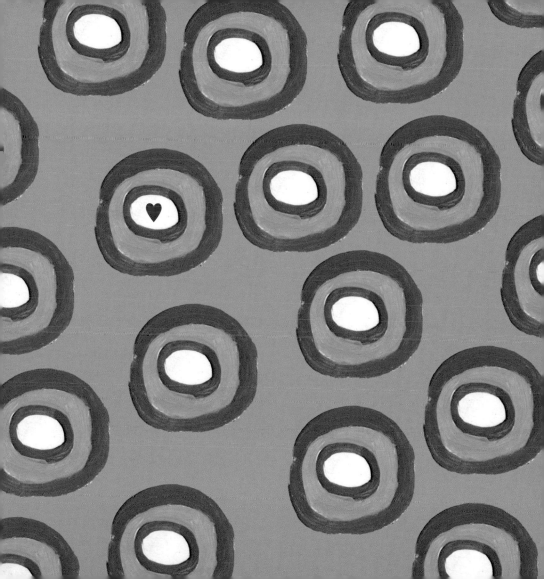

Make time for the important stuff.

Piggyback rides. Hopscotch.

Collecting bugs. Underdogs.

Mud pies. Freeze tag.

Drawing on the sidewalk.

Making a wish. Climbing trees.

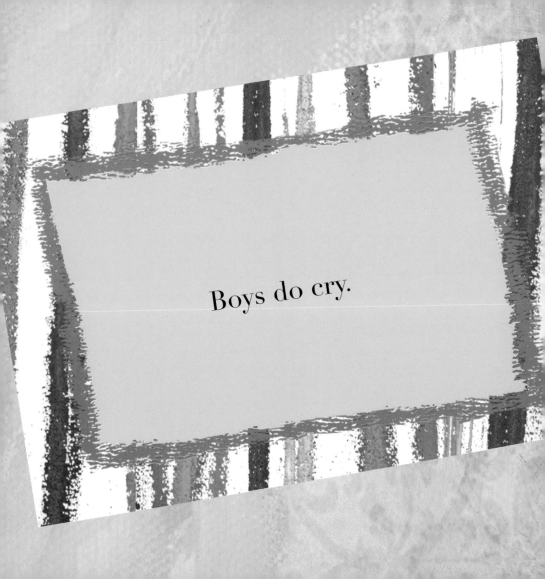

Boys do cry.

And it's a good thing.

It shows they are complex
and sensitive and
not so tough after all.

Cherish the journey and
the adventure of parenthood.

The gifts will be many,
the lessons innumerable,
the love all consuming.

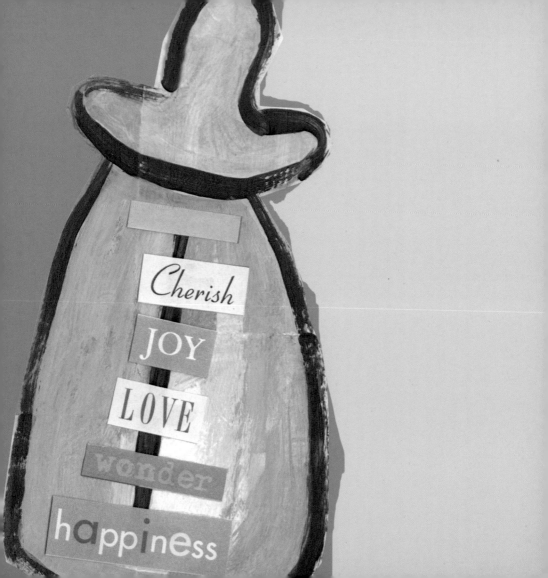

Cherish

JOY

LOVE

wonder

happiness

What an *incredible* blessing.

About the Author

Beloved author and artist Marianne Richmond has touched the lives of millions for nearly two decades through her award-winning books, greeting cards, and other gift products that offer people the most heartfelt way to connect with each other. She lives in the Minneapolis area. Visit www.mariannerichmond.com.